CAUGHT IN ACTION

20 YEARS OF WEST INDIES CRICKET PHOTOGRAPHY
BY GORDON BROOKS

Published by Wordsmith International

Marketed and Distributed by Miller Publishing Company
Edgehill, St. Thomas, Barbados, West Indies.
Tel: (246) 421-6700 . Fax: (246) 421-6707 . Email: miller@caribsurf.com

Printed in Canada

ISBN 976 - 8079 - 74 - 6

DEDICATED TO THE MEMORY

OF

CYPRIAN LATOUCHE JR.

MY FRIEND & PARTNER

CONTENTS

THE introductions to each section and all the photo-captions have been written by Tony Cozier, West Indies' most successful, highly respected and world renowned cricket commentator.

GORDON BROOKS
A Distinguished Sort of a Cricket Person

AT THE START of play he inevitably emerges from the players' pavilion just before the umpires take up their positions. Nonchalantly, but with purpose, he shuffles to either third man or fine leg, but shifts position depending on the state of the game. Gordon Brooks is the enduring cricket photographer whose all-seeing eye is as sharp as Gordon Greenidge's was, whose temperament is as cool as Geoff Boycott's and whose record is as varied and prolific as Gary Sobers'.

Born to island photographer Clarence Brooks and his wife Elmont, a camera was never out of Gordon's sight. When he became apprenticed to his father and Cyprian LaTouche at the Barbados Advocate as a photoengraver, he learned quickly the finer points involved in using metal to reproduce the dots that would transform a picture into print for the paper. In 1971 he opened Brooks LaTouche Photography with partner Cyprian LaTouche Jr. with whom he had done many photographic exploits for the newspaper. A largely commercial photography enterprise, Gordon soon began taking pictures for the NATION newspaper which he helped found two years later.

One thing led to another, and soon he was doing overseas assignments with investigative journalists like Al Gilkes and Charles Harding, chasing Hurricane David in Dominica; gun runner Sydney Burnett-Alleyne in Martinique and indeed the entire Grenada revolution from protest in 1979 to the murder of Prime Minister Maurice Bishop four years later.

More and more he showed interest in cricket photography until in 1984 Tony Cozier, the leading Caribbean cricket writer and broadcaster, suggested to Gordon he should undertake an international tour. Within weeks he was off to cover the West Indies tour of England. He has done every single tour there since; two visits to Australia and one to South Africa, the first official tour of a West Indies team.

Gordon Brooks readily admits his game started as innocently as any cricketer's would have in the modesty of domestic competition. He readily admits that his early fare was often just umpires making their way to the centre, captains tossing the coin, batsmen striding to or from the pitch, or the team entering or leaving the field.

But this book, **Caught in Action,** tells a different story. It shares pictures of test match quality. The still shot that freezes cricket's best and most famous moments for all time and for all the glory. An umpire's upraised finger of finality in the background and out of focus and the despairing batsman looking on in awe, but very much in focus. The moment of fear as a tall, gangling fast bowler makes his menacing emergence behind the umpire at the point of ball release, seen from the crouching perspective of an anxious, helmeted batsman, padded all over, 22 short yards away.

He has used everything from 300 to 600 mm lenses and the monstrous three-foot Big Bertha to today's palm-sized digital camera to capture for posterity the microsecond when the ball makes contact with the palm of the hand of a player in mid-air; or the fancy footwork of a ballet artist with a cricket bat in hand.

Gordon credits British photographers Patrick Egar and Adrian Murrell with giving him the insights and support to develop into an internationally-recognised cricket photographer; and Trinidadian Roy Boyke and Willie Alleyne of Barbados for inspiring him to make a career out of newspaper photography.

What makes Gordon Brooks' work great is no different from what makes batsmen legendary. In his own words he identifies the following as the keys to his success, He said: "You need to know and understand the game; you must have the ability to concentrate for long periods; you must know how to position yourself; and you must have good hand and eye co-ordination." No batsman goes very far in the game without these attributes.

No wonder that long after praise for the Caribbean's exhilarating cricket died at the end of the 1980s, Gordon continues to reap plaudits for his own exploits. And he continues to enjoy the human pleasure of relations he has developed with people in far-flung places.

The gregarious guy that Gordon is, you must believe that cricket tours are not just long days in the sun and hard nights in the darkroom. His assignments have brought him friends he never would have met and times he cannot forget. Ask him, for instance, to explain what it is like to spend Christmas as far as it is possible to be away from the Caribbean, in Australia. For that he thanks people in Victoria like the Turks and the Damsons, who reached out to him and who have become lifelong friends. Cricket assignments have embellished his career; the tours have enriched his life. For Gordon to have devoted all his years to carving out his niche in Caribbean cricket record-keeping, he must have loved the game very dearly. For him to have used his lens so adeptly to poignantly capture the essentials and the exploits of our players, he must have had some perspective and context of the value of the game to our people.

Gordon Brooks therefore joins the company of outstanding persons like E. W. Swanton who saw and shared the glory of the game almost exclusively from beyond the boundary. Gordon Brooks: A distinguished Sort of a Cricket Person. ■

HAROLD HOYTE,
Editor in Chief, The Nation Newspaper, Barbados

A MASTER OF HIS ART
Just Beyond The Boundary

LONG BEFORE Gordon Brooks exploded into the global public view he was quietly a part of mine. A few people in Barbados would know that we are sons of the 'Ivy', a suburb on the southeastern perimeter of Bridgetown, and that we attended the distinguished St. Giles Primary School where I was his senior by two years. Like my older brother he began his career in journalism in his mid-teens with the Barbados Advocate; Llewellyn as a printer and Gordon as a photographer. That was in the early 1950s when I imagined myself a wicketkeeper-opening batsman and had not made my first class debut as a fast bowler. He remains until today an intimate part of our family.

When the quintessential Caribbean cricket writer, the late CLR James, coined the term 'beyond a boundary' in 1957 as a way of seeing and knowing the culture of the game, his gaze was entirely sociological. The lens he used was that of the literary and creative artist. He saw more than most but knew that it was less than what there was. In the same year I wore the West Indies maroon cap for the first time. It was the tour to England but Gordon had already established himself as a gifted artist on the 1955 Australian tour to the West Indies.

This book by Brooks, a compilation of some of the best photography of West Indies cricket that exists, serves to complete the story of a great West Indian journey to excellence. The images Gordon has made available to us belong, therefore, to a different tradition of expression. His vantage point, as close to the boundary as it is possible to be, is that of the talking eye which has seen more than most can imagine. Through him we are invited to share the magic West Indies players have given the world during the second half of the last century.

Gordon Brooks is not just a great Caribbean cricket photographer; he is an artist with a powerful mind who has used his imagination to tell one of the greatest tales of the modern world. He chose to dedicate a life to this visual art, and to a topic that requires the finest of minds and the sharpest of eyes. Before his camera could capture the genius of the greats who gave excellence to West Indies performance, it had to be first imagined and understood. His lens gave life to the lore, and the results are here in this fine collection that has no peer.

Think about the dimensions of this effort. West Indies cricketers, from Learie to Lara, rescued the test match from a theatrically dull, democratically destitute 19th century world with an enormous injection of artistry, athleticism, and social accessibility. The investment made by the post-war generation of battling battalions of the 3Ws, Sobers and Kanhai, Rowe and Richards, and Greenidge and Haynes to the bowling ballistics of doomsday couples such as Griffith and the "other chap", Roberts and Holding, Garner and Marshall, and Walsh and Ambrose, constitute a cultural legacy unmatched anywhere, anytime.

Gordon could very well have been blinded by the beauty and magnificence of it all. Instead he steadied his hand, knitted his brow, and became its speaking eye. This book is in part a celebration of great artists by one who bore witness, but it is more, much more. It is a monument dedicated to a message, a simple truth, which says that great things can be found in small places among people who more often than not had less than enough. It is a book of pictures that tells this large, unrelenting truth.

This is how we have come to know and read Gordon's images. To capture the truth and set it free is the way of the genuine artist. It is how we know that there is a difference between doing it for love and love doing it. There is a whole lot of love going on in these photos; this is the emotion that runs through the veins when you view them. It is because you cannot see them on the surface; you are pulled in, under the skin, to feel the stir in the spirit that drives and sustains West Indies cricket. It is art at its finest, like a song hummed during the endurance of trouble.

These photos, then, are not for the eyes only. They are for those who know that there is more to it than meets the eye. What we have here are insights into the souls of soldiers in the field. It is a narrative told in the movements of arms and legs, minds and muscles, heads and hearts. This gives meaning to the words of the legendary CLR James when he asserts that:

> "Cricket is a game and must be compared with other games
> Cricket is an art and must be compared with other arts
> With ballet, drama and dance".

This is what Gordon has captured, as we see insights into the minds of a nation with its mind made up, the arts of batting, bowling and fielding are here displayed the West Indian way and for this we must thank the little master who for a life time crouched beyond the boundary. ■

REV. WES HALL, GCM, HBM, JP.
President, West Indies Cricket Board

CAUGHT IN ACTION
A Treasure Trove of Memories

TO HAVE BEEN considered as one worthy of presenting an introduction for this epic work of such historical significance to West Indies cricket, and indeed the West Indian culture, is a rare honor. Having observed the consistently high quality of his photography ever since the early days of my career, I have always thought of Gordon Brooks as no less a professional than those whom he has so artistically captured in this still, yet moving documentary.

In effect, this collection of pictures explodes with the power of a Vivian Richards, the panache of a Brian Lara, and the poignant penetrativeness of a Malcolm Marshall.

The 20 years of West Indian cricket represented in this book covers a fascinating period that saw the regional team go from a euphoric state of domination in international cricket from the mid-70s through the 80s, to a condition of steady decline from the mid-90s, to a period of transition at the dawn of the 21st century. For me it had been an exhilarating experience to be on the cutting edge of leadership that developed arguably the most dominant team ever in cricket. Conversely, to have witnessed from my vantage point, the debacle that was the first Test series between West Indies and South Africa, was the nadir.

The South Africa sojourn was unsavory not only because of the humiliating defeat but also because it was an embarrassment to have performed so poorly before much of the non-white population who, hereto, had revered the achievements of some of our greatest cricketers. Having been a great admirer of President Nelson Mandela - a unique human being who, in his quest to free a people, did not allow himself to be burdened by the weight of historical injustice; a man whose lifetime of struggles and triumphs has touched so many of us beyond the borders of South Africa – it would have been a source of immense pride to have been even moderately successful on the tour.

Many of the never-before-seen photographs that adorn this landmark publication reflect the fun, excitement and the ebullience of men playing a boy's game on a field of dreams that stretches from Bridgetown to Bangalore, Port-of-Spain to Port Elizabeth, from London to Lahore and from St. John's to Sydney. But most importantly this spectacular pictorial presents a mosaic of a game that transcends its boundaries to unify and elevate the Caribbean community as no other sport, cultural or political entity has done.

To quote the late Prime Minister of Jamaica, Michael Manley, "Cricket is the most completely regional activity undertaken by the people of CARICOM. It is also the most successful co-operative endeavor and, as such, is a constant reminder to a people of otherwise wayward insularity of the value of collaboration."

It is this notion that inspired my ambition, as did the legacy of Sir Frank Worrell, when I had the honor to serve as captain of the West Indies. Sir Frank's grace, his dignity and astuteness in leadership, as well as his relentless pursuit of equality and fair play, provided a blue print for my stewardship. My goals were mainly to rekindle team spirit, to dispel our endemic cavalier image and to establish a winning attitude.

As we embarked on our mission, it was our good fortune that we were blessed with a cadre of talented young players. However, the team's success was more than just a matter of luck. And if it were indeed luck, it would have been an acronym for Labor Under Correct Knowledge.

Shrewdness that would have grown from countless seasons on the English County Cricket and international circuit that provided ample opportunity, not just to compete under variable conditions but to keenly observe techniques and tendencies of thousands of players. And also insights gleaned from past players such as Sir Garfield Sobers, Rohan Kanhai, Lance Gibbs, Basil Butcher, Seymore Nurse, Wes Hall and others.

'Caught in Action' brings into sharp focus the outstanding individual efforts that are cumulatively responsible for West Indies record-breaking success. With a keen sense of timing, Gordon Brooks has assembled in his book a veritable honor roll of super heroes who should be enshrined in a West Indies Hall of Fame. Some of the distinguished colleagues whose superb achievements remain timeless and formidable are Gordon Greenidge and Desmond Haynes- perhaps the best opening pair in the history of cricket; the late Roy Fredericks, maybe the most mentally tough player that I have ever known; Viv Richards, who with skilled bravado took the art of batsmanship to a whole new level; the ever dependable Alvin Kallicharan, Larry Gomes and Jeffrey Dujon; world record holder Brian Lara and Richie Richardson: and that incomparable phalanx of fast bowlers, Andy Roberts, Michael Holding, Malcolm Marshall, Joel Garner, Colin Croft, Courtney Walsh and Curtly Ambrose.

For the multitude of West Indies cricket fans throughout the world, who have ridden the proverbial roller-coaster and lived vicariously through their heroes, this book is a valuable resource and a treasure trove of memories. As someone who has been involved with West Indies cricket for all of my adult life, 'Caught in Action' is an important initiative that is long overdue.

Conceptually, it reminds us all of the monumental efforts of gifted athletes who would wear the burgundy cap with pride and passion and commitment. Some far too quickly fade from view and are forgotten. Quintessential team players that routinely turned pressure into adrenaline and flaunted their mental toughness with almost an arrogant flair- like all of the afore-named, and the likes of Lester King, Keith Boyce, Charlie Davis, Winston Davis and others.

'Caught in Action' complements the precious few literary works that accurately chronicle West Indies cricket; those books that serve to inform young aspiring cricketers around the Caribbean who would be inspired by the legend of Malcolm Marshall when he defied logic and demolished England in the third Test at Leeds in 1984, taking 7 for 53 with one hand broken and in a cast.

I am confident that this book, which intrinsically preserves the rich tradition of West Indies cricket, will not only be well received in the Caribbean but by cricket fans the world over. ■

CLIVE H. LLOYD

1981-1985

GORDON BROOKS chose an opportune time to turn his photographic expertise to the coverage of West Indies cricket. No team has ever dominated the game quite so comprehensively as the West Indies did through the decade of the 1980s – and never more so than in the years to 1985 when Clive Lloyd ended his tenure as their longest-serving and most successful captain.

After narrow and contentious defeat in a series in New Zealand early in 1980, that they were convinced owed more to biased umpiring than cricketing merit, they won 21 of 42 Tests played, in Australia, England, Australia and India as well as the Caribbean. They succumbed only twice, both on turning pitches at the Sydney Cricket Ground on separate tours of Australia.

Gordon was absent on the three losing occasions, in New Zealand and Australia, as he was for the shock of the defeat by India in the 1983 World Cup final at Lord's. He had not yet begun following the West Indies to distant lands, so he recorded only West Indian successes in that time. Indeed, between 1978, against Australia, and 1990, against England, the West Indies did not lose a single Test at home.

The statistics were breathtaking. Of the 21 victories prior to Lloyd's retirement, seven were by an innings. In 1984, the West Indies went six consecutive Tests (all five against Australia in the Caribbean and the first in the summer in England) without losing a second innings wicket. When the sequence was broken, at Lord's in the second Test against England, the only wicket was through a run out. Nothing ever seemed impossible, no cause ever lost.

With India 164 ahead and four second innings standing at tea on the final day of the first Test in 1983, the crowd at Sabina Park foresaw an obvious draw and began to drift out towards home. In the first over on resumption, Andy Roberts removed three wickets, the last fell two overs later and the West Indies were left with 172 to win off 26 overs, a rate of 6.6 runs an over.

It was an equation only a team as super-confident as Lloyd's would have given thought to. With Viv Richards to the fore, as he so frequently was, punching 61 off 35 balls, the goal was achieved with four wickets and four balls remaining. The West Indies expunged the unaccustomed complacency that led to their 1983 World Cup final demise at Lord's against the same opponents a few months later, going to India and pounding their erstwhile conquerors 3-0 in the Tests and 6-1 in the one-day internationals.

When David Gower delayed his declaration of England's second innings until early on the last morning at Lord's in 1984, it seemed unnecessary timidity for which he was widely castigated. It was regarded more a chance for England's bowlers to press for victory over the remaining four and a half hours, plus the mandatory 20 overs in the final hour, than a realistic challenge for the West Indies batsmen to make the necessary 344 for victory.

True to their convictions, Gordon Greenidge blazed an unbeaten 214, the solid left-hander Larry Gomes a supportive 92 in an unbroken second wicket partnership of 287 and the West Indies completed their mission with as many as 11.5 overs and nine wickets to spare. It was the second victory in the first of two 5-0 clean sweeps, the so-called "blackwashes", over England in the decade.

In Barbados a few months earlier, Australia had accumulated 429 batting first – and still lost by 10 wickets. These were all part of 11 consecutive Test victories that year, an unprecedented sequence in the game's history until Australia reeled off 16 in a row seven years later.

The basis of such excellence was the quality of the players who were fired by a strong sense of purpose and commitment and a professionalism honed in English county and league cricket and developed in the two seasons of Kerry Packer's fiercely competitive, high-standard World Series Cricket in Australia. Few teams of any era could match the power of Lloyd's at its zenith.

If spin bowling was generally non-existent, it was redundant in an attack mounted on feared, and fearsome, pace. The eleven who annihilated Australia by an innings and 112 runs in Perth and by eight wickets in the first two Tests in Brisbane in 1985-85 were typical. They were, in batting order, Gordon Greenidge, Desmond Haynes, Richie Richardson, Gomes, Richards, Lloyd, Jeffrey Dujon, Malcolm Marshall, Michael Holding, Joel Garner and Courtney Walsh.

All but Richardson and Walsh, then at the start of their lengthy careers, were at the peak of their powers. Greenidge and Haynes were the most durable opening pair in Test history, Richards and Lloyd two of the most commanding batsmen of all time and Gomes the ideal foil to the stroke-makers around him. Dujon was indisputably the finest wicket-keeper/batsman the West Indies have produced. Marshall, Holding, Garner and Walsh – whose Test wickets would total 1,403 at the end of their days - the relentless pace attack.

These were halcyon days for West Indies cricket that filled all West Indians with a sense of pride and joy – and provided Gordon Brooks with a host of indelible images. ∎

THE spectacular climax, in the middle and on the boundary, to Michael Holding's fearsome opening over to Geoffrey Boycott in England's first innings of the Kensington Oval Test. "In his fourteen and a half years of Test cricket the venerable Boycott could have encountered no six consecutive deliveries like them," the West Indies Cricket Annual recorded. "The sixth, well up, found Boycott's feet and bat virtually transfixed and the off-stump was sent spectacularly cartwheeling 20 yards towards the wicket-keeper. There was spontaneous cartwheeling among the spectators as well as sheer bedlam broke out."

ENGLAND had an especially difficult time on their tour, on and off the field. It was in danger of cancellation when Robin Jackman was expelled from Guyana because of his contacts with South Africa. When it did resume, with the third Test in Barbados, Jackman dismissed Gordon Greenidge with his fifth ball in Test cricket and Desmond Haynes (above) in his sixth over. That night, things took a turn for the worse with the death of England's assistant manager, the former Test batsman Ken Barrington, from a heart attack and Viv Richards added to the misery with an unbeaten 182 in the second innings that included several trademark shots (right).

THE dos and dont's of slip catching. Everton Mattis gets body and hands in the right position to snare England's David Bairstow off Michael Holding in the Kensington Oval Test of 1981 while India's Sunil Gavaskar gets both out of the way to avoid Desmond Haynes' top edged cut against India at the same ground two years later.

THERE was no braver batting against the hostile West Indies' fast bowling in the 1980s than Mohinder Amarnath's on India's 1983 tour. Like several of his teammates, he took blows to head and body – as in the fourth Test at Kensington Oval (above left) when he missed his hook and was cut on the mouth. But he remained unbowed to amass a tour aggregate of 598 runs at an average of 66.44. The West Indies took the series 2-0, their bowlers supported by catches such as Clive Lloyd's off Kapil Dev and wicket-keeper Jeffrey Dujon's off Sunil Gavaskar in the same Test.

THE skippers in the 1983 series, Clive Lloyd of the West Indies and Kapil Dev of India, leave the field after Lloyd won the toss in the second Test at the Queen's Park Oval. When the West Indies batted second, Lloyd came in with Greenidge, Haynes and Richards all gone with a single on the board and (above) compiled a vital 143 in a stand of 237 with Larry Gomes. Kapil responded with a match-saving, unbeaten 100 in India's second innings. In the last series of his magnificent career, Andy Roberts (right) claimed 24 wickets at an average of 22.7.

THE West Indies were at the zenith of their powers in 1984, defeating Australia 3-0 at home and 3-1 away and handing England the first of two so-called 'blackwashes', 5-0 in England. In the final Test against Australia at Sabina, Australia's wicket-keeper Wayne Phillips edged Joel Garner to his opposite number, Jeffrey Dujon, but proved that sharp catching was not a West Indian preserve with his tumbling take to account for Roger Harper off John Macguire in the same Test.

RICHIE Richardson (left, above) and Viv Richards on their way out at the Recreation Ground in their native Antigua to resume their third wicket partnership of 308 in the fourth Test against Australia in 1984. In his first Test in his native island, Richardson scored 154. Richards' 178 was his second hundred on the ground. Earlier, in the first Test at Bourda, Clive Lloyd, catching Kepler Wessels at slip off Joel Garner, and the leaping wicket-keeper Jeffrey Dujon displayed the agility of Olympic gymnasts.

WATCHED from beyond Bourda's Regent Street canal by the intrepid tree dwellers (below left), Desmond Haynes sneaks runs past gully on his way to his second innings hundred in the first Test against Australia (top left) and (right) Jeffrey Dujon loses his cap, but not the ball, in catching Steve Smith off Joel Garner. In the fifth Test at Sabina, Alan Border's edge off Malcolm Marshall (above) was more straightforward but the appeal just as animated.

IT was a tough summer for David Gower. He was the second England captain, after Johnnie Douglas against Australia in 1920-21, to lose all five Tests of a series. As a batsman, he fell lbw to Malcolm Marshall for 3 in the first innings at Lord's (above) and averaged a mere 19. In spite of England's innings loss and his own bowling figures of one for 127 in the first Test at Edgbaston, Ian Botham could share a laugh with his great friend Viv Richards, who had just made 117.

PERHAPS the most remarkable of all the West Indies' triumphs in their period of domination was at Lord's in 1984. England declared with nine wickets down on the last day to allow their bowlers to press their seeming advantage. Instead, the West Indies turned the tables and romped home by scoring 344 for the solitary loss of Desmond Haynes through a run out with 11.5 overs to spare. Gordon Greenidge unleashed 29 fours, among them a cut off Derek Pringle (right) in an unbeaten 214. He and Larry Gomes, 92, shared a stand of 287 and the pair could celebrate a famous victory afterwards with the best champagne.

1985-1991

THE Clive Lloyd Era ended with the disappointment of an unbecoming defeat by Australia at the Sydney Cricket Ground in January, 1985, only his 12th loss in 74 Tests under his command. His 36 victories remain the most of any Test captain in the game's history.

The Viv Richards Era began the following March, with the first Test against New Zealand at the Queen's Park Oval. When it ended, six and a half years later, also in a rare defeat, against England at the Oval in London, Richards had led the West Indies to 27 victories against eight losses in 50 Tests, the only West Indies captain never to be conquered in a series. Their styles of leadership were as different as their personalities - Lloyd's calm, composed and understated; Richards' assertive, commanding and confident. The one salient similarity was that they both led from the front, imposing as aggressive batsmen, motivational as skippers.

Unlike Lloyd, Richards had to contend with the disruptive team changes. As key players aged together, some went into early retirement. The consistency of those who stayed on understandably waned. Such a transition often placed the proud West Indies record in jeopardy but, somehow, they found the resilience to maintain it. There was no immediate indication of the struggles that intermittently followed. New Zealand were duly despatched 2-0 in the Caribbean in Richards' first go at the helm and England subjected to the same 5-0 humiliation on their 1986 Caribbean tour they had suffered in England two years earlier. The two victories over New Zealand were by 10 wickets as were two against England to add to another by an innings. In those nine Tests, the West Indies were not dismissed for less than 300 in any innings. Always one to seize the moment, Richards embellished the second "blackwash" by blasting six sixes and seven fours in compiling Test cricket's most hectic hundred, off 56 balls, in the final Test at the Antigua Recreation Ground. It was an emphatic cricketing statement to end a series once more overshadowed by anti-apartheid protests against the presence of players with South African connections in the England team. The early results gave the impression that the West Indian dominance of the world game would be everlasting. It was an illusion.

Over the next two years, they were hard-pressed to keep their opponents at bay. Pakistan pressed them to earn 1-1 series splits in Pakistan in 1986 and in the Caribbean in 1988. New Zealand held them 1-1 in New Zealand early in 1987, as India did in India at the end of the year. In the same period, they failed to reach the final of the World Cup for the first time, falling at the first round of the tournament in India and Pakistan. Each time, the team was diminished by stalwart absentees. Michael Holding and Joel Garner opted out of the trip to Pakistan. A year later, they and the dependable Larry Gomes simultaneously drew the curtains on their distinguished careers. Marshall, requesting "an overdue break", missed India. The World Cup campaign was undertaken without all four and without Gordon Greenidge as well. Such changes brought new players into the team and put the burden on others already there.

Richie Richardson and Carl Hooper, who were introduced under Lloyd, established themselves as batsmen of the future. Courtney Walsh, another nurtured in Lloyd's later days, gradually developed from a persevering, into-the-wind support fast bowler into one of the spearheads of the attack. Curtly Ambrose and Ian Bishop needed no such measured transformation. From their initial series (Ambrose against Pakistan in 1988, Bishop against India a year later), they established themselves as worthy successors to those they replaced.

By the summer of 1988, the West Indies' juggernaut was rolling on all cylinders again. Away from home, England were once more trounced, 4-0, in the summer of 1988 when they used four different captains, and Australia were on the receiving end of a similarly familiar defeat, 3-1, when Lloyd returned as manager to resume his association with the team he had helped build. Back in the Caribbean in the 1989 season, India went under 3-0. With Marshall to the fore, the pace attack was irresistible, even if the batting was not quite as formidable as it once was. In the 14 relevant Tests, Marshall, Ambrose and Walsh collected 165 wickets between them, 68 to Marshall at less than 20 runs each.

The team was so settled that only 12 players were used in the series in Australia and in the West Indies against India. The earlier hiccups seemed no more than a passing phase – but they were to return before Richards bade his emotional farewell to Test cricket at London's Oval in August 1991. After a stunning upset by nine wickets in the first Test at Sabina Park, England might well have taken the series in the Caribbean in 1990 but for the weather than denied them a likely victory at the Queen's Park Oval and the sensational intervention of Ambrose late on the final day at Kensington that drew the West Indies level.

So inspired, the deal was sealed by an innings triumph in the last Test when Greenidge and Haynes accumulated the highest of their opening partnerships, a West Indies' record 298. There was a 1-1 result in Pakistan late in 1990 when Richards, incapacitated by an operation for hemorrhoids, handed over temporary control to Haynes. A 2-1 decision over Australia in the Caribbean followed and, finally under Richards, a hard-fought 2-2-2 split of the six Tests in England that summer. The closing stages of Richards' term was marred by controversy, much of it fired by his own no-nonsense competitiveness. He himself stormed into the press box to berate an English journalist while his team was in the field in the Antigua Test of 1990. Next season, when Australia toured, umpires reported the abusive language of certain players on the field and the respective boards became involved in a succession of verbal exchanges after Richards' critical comments on Australian coach Bob Simpson. The situation was such that then West Indies Cricket Board president, Clyde Walcott, voiced his concern over the soured relations between the teams.

It made a refreshing change when Wisden wrote of the 1991 tour of England, Richards' last: "The series was even more attractive for being staged in the best of spirits without the bad blood which sullied the Australian visit to the West Indies earlier in the year." Richards, as devastating a batsman and as powerful a personality as the game has known, fittingly received glowing tributes after he announced the Oval Test was his last. A celebrated period of West Indies cricket was at an end. ■

THE Richards Era began in 1985 following the retirement of Clive Lloyd, aged 40 – but nothing much changed. Batsmen, like New Zealand's Jeremy Coney (above) and Ken Rutherford, still had to keep evading bouncers from Malcolm Marshall and Joel Garner in the home series of 1985.....

.....there were still the high-fives to celebrate regular wickets, Jeffrey Dujon leapt about behind the wicket as he always did to grasp edged catches and Gordon Greenidge's trademark pull was still in working order, as against Ian Botham in the Queen's Park Oval Test against England in 1986.

JOY unrestrained at the Antigua Recreation Ground during the 1986 Test. Bowler Roger Harper and captain Viv Richards whoop it up at the dismissal of Ian Botham while the on-field antics of local characters, the handstanding "Gravy" and the more sedate "Crocus", leave England fielder Wayne Larkins nonplussed.

THE resident mutt 'supervises' the between-innings rolling at the Queen's Park Oval, preparing the pitch for another start to the West Indies' innings by the most durable opening pair in the game's history, Gordon Greenidge and Desmond Haynes. During their long and fruitful association, they combined in 89 Tests, more than double any pairing from any country, had 16 century partnerships and averaged 47.32 per wicket.

LIKE all champions, Viv Richards possessed an uncanny sense of occasion, never more evident than in his performances in his native St.John's at the Antigua Recreation Ground where he had first made his reputation. He celebrated his island's inaugural Test, in 1981 against England, with his marriage to Miriam in a ceremony fit for royalty just two days prior to the match and an inevitable hundred, 114, in the West Indies innings. Three years later, there was another special innings, 178, to mark Australia's first Test on the ground. And, in 1986, in his first Test as captain in Antigua, he and his countrymen had further cause for rejoicing when he recorded a hundred off fewer balls than had ever been done in Test history. When he acknowledged his landmark with raised bat and broad smile, he had faced only 56 balls and hit six sixes and seven fours, adding another six for good measure before declaring at 110 not out.

DEATH TO THE RACIST SOUTH AFRICAN REGIME!

THE UN SAY

RAE LEQUAY STOLLMEYER AGENTS OF BOTHA IN THE CARIBBEAN

FOR their second successive tour, England – and the leaders of the West Indies Cricket Board of Control for accepting them - attracted the ire of anti-apartheid protesters incensed by the presence of players with South African connections in the team. On the field, they had a miserable time, beaten in all five Tests in spite of the occasional belligerence of Ian Botham, seen hooking his former Somerset teammate Joel Garner at the Antigua Recreation Ground.

"CAPTAIN, the ship is sinking," a popular calypso of the day with a political bent, was converted by unkind West Indians into a theme for the beleaguered David Gower as England slumped to their second successive 5-0 thrashing. Two of the causes were Patrick Patterson, a new fearsome addition to the West Indies' fast bowling arsenal (left) and the more familiar Joel Garner making Gower bob and weave at the Queen's Park Oval, (right).

HAPPINESS for leaping Pakistani off-spinner Shoail Mohammed was a cracked Bourda pitch and a West Indian wicket on the way to victory in the first Test. But the ultimate joy was West Indian as their hugging ninth wicket pair, Jeffrey Dujon (right) and Winston Benjamin, took them to a victory by two wickets in the last Test at Kensington Oval to clinch the series.

THE end for Mike Gatting – in more ways than one. The England captain was snapped up by Gus Logie off Malcolm Marshall in the first innings of the first Test and then sacked following allegations in the tabloid press of his nocturnal relationship with a young waitress during the match. England proceeded to lose the next four Tests – in the face of West Indian team spirit evidenced by Jeffrey Dujon and his shorter partner, Logie, during their vital stand of 130 at Lord's and in spite of Desmond Haynes' temporary discomfort against Derek Pringle (right).

NO more intimidating sight for a bowler, Viv Richards explodes with a typical shot over mid-wicket during his 80 in the first Test against England at Trent Bridge. There was a rare failure for Desmond Haynes at Lord's where he had compiled his highest Test score, 184, eight years earlier. This time he was snapped up by the tumbling Martin Moxon for 8 in the first innings.

AN exciting new fast bowler, Ian Bishop, announced his arrival against India with a six-wickets haul in his second Test at Kensington Oval. The first of what were to be 161 wickets in a career cruelly ended by chronic back problems was Arun Lal, caught behind for 8 (above, left). The rain ruined first test at Bourda, Richie Richardson compiled his highest of 16 Test centuries, 194, using his favourite square-cut to beneficial effect (above, right). England proved tougher opponents the following season and it needed Curtly Ambrose's eight second innings wickets at Kensington, among them Jack Russell bowled for a gutsy 55, to level the series 1-1 before victory in the last Test clinched it 2-1.

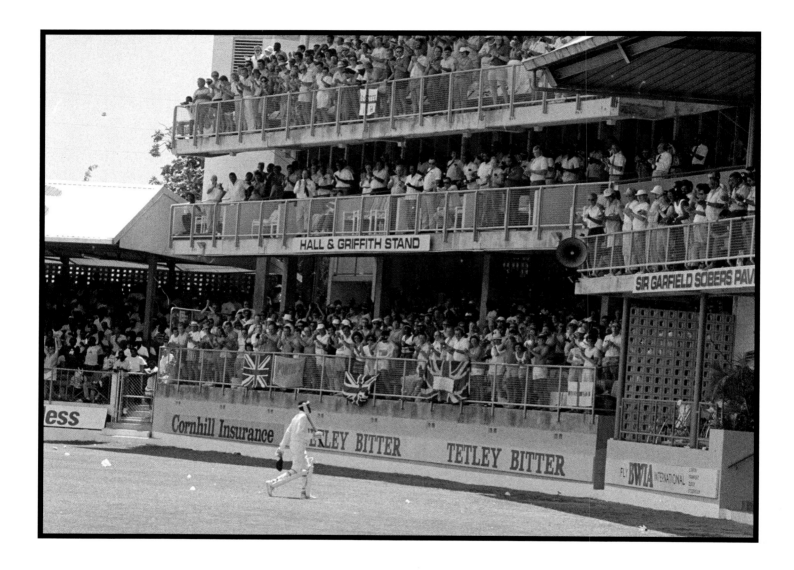

DELIGHT and distress for Carlisle Best, the Barbadian batsman, in his first Test series. Floored when hit where it hurts most during the Sabina Park Test, he got a helping hand from England's sympathetic wicket-keeper Jack Russell. In his native Barbados, the hand he got came from appreciative spectators, West Indian and English, as he left the ground after his magnificent 164.

FAMILIAR images of West Indies cricket. At Kensington Oval, senior groundsmen Hendy Davis and the late Livingstone "Boo" Medford, have a young helper in their wake as they head to the middle with their pitch preparation paraphernalia. At the Queen's Park Oval, the late Russell "Blue Food" Keller's conch-shell was a clarion call for the West Indies. And, everywhere, an opposition wicket has always been guaranteed to prompt a gyrating reaction.

THE defining moment in the series. With England needing 151 to win the third Test and to stretch their lead to 2-0, Graham Gooch takes an excruciating blow on the hand from a ball from Ezra Moseley. Even a cursory, on the spot examination can diagnose a broken bone. With their captain and leading batsman out, England lost the last two Tests and the series.

THREE unusual sights during the series. Confused England batsman David Capel pleads for instructions from the team hierarchy in the pavilion in the closing stages of the third Test – keep on going after the winning target of 151 or accept the umpires' offer of fading light? The latter came back as the answer, leaving the match drawn. In the one-day international at the Queen's Park Oval and the first Test at Sabina, Viv Richards had his stumps hit by England bowlers of West Indian birth – Gladstone Small (above) and Devon Malcolm (right).

DESERVING, if unusual, acclaim for a dazzling hundred as elated Bourda fans hail Richie Richardson on the way to his 182 in the second Test against Australia. Wearing the broad-brimmed sunhat that was his trademark, Richardson shows off the nimble footwork of a cricketing Michael Jackson during his 104 against England at Edgbaston that summer.

ANOTHER wicket for Courtney Walsh, a scar of battle for Gus Logie and a boundary for Desmond Haynes during the tough, uncompromising home series against Australia. Walsh celebrates his first-ball victim in the last Test in Antigua but Mark Waugh can't bear to face the umpire's inevitable lbw decision. Bloodied but unbowed after he was felled by Craig McDermott's bouncer, the plastered Logie bravely resumed with seven stitches in the wound to topscore with 77 not out in the first Test at Sabina Park where Haynes and wicket-keeper Ian Healy renewed close quarter acquaintances.

RIVAL fans show their appreciation to their heroes in different ways during the Antigua Test. The young Australians wave their flag and genuflect to century-maker Mark Taylor; the omnipresent "doctor" Gravy and bare backed assistant checks on the health of the West Indians as they leave the field.

1992-1995

ALL good things must come to an end. For the West Indies, the decisive date was May 3, 1995, the luckless location Sabina Park and the relevant result an innings and 53 runs loss to Australia that closed the longest period of dominance world cricket has known.

For 15 years, the West Indies had maintained an unmatched record of invincibility in Test series of varying duration but it had become increasingly tenuous. Six of the 13 contested under Viv Richards' captaincy were drawn and it was only a powerful self-belief, a legacy of their immediate past, and the presence of a pair of remarkable fast bowlers, Curtly Ambrose and Courtney Walsh, that kept the opposition at bay for another four years after Richards played his final Test. The hand-over of the captaincy to another Antiguan, Richie Richardson, prior to the 1992 World Cup, was overshadowed by the kind of controversy that was to become commonplace.

Although he formally retired from Test cricket after the 1991 England tour, Richards made it known he was available and eager to take his leave of the international stage in the World Cup, in Australia and New Zealand. But he was not chosen by selectors wary of the effect his imposing presence might have on his new successor. Gordon Greenidge and Jeffrey Dujon were also omitted, bringing their stellar careers to an end and diminishing the experience and strength Richardson would have under him. Such decisions did not sit easily with either the individuals themselves, or the passionate public, and when Malcolm Marshall, another champion from the Lloyd-Richards Eras, joined them in retirement after the World Cup, he left stating he "never felt part" of Richardson's team and complaining of his "shabby" treatment. Marshall's remarks were generally interpreted at the time as sour grapes. But they would return to haunt West Indies cricket. "Everything seems to be going down the drain," he observed. "There is no respect, no manners."

What followed under Richardson – and, for a brief period when fatique obliged him to rest and hand over to the admirable Walsh - were a succession of great escapes inspired by Ambrose and Walsh, a couple of monumental performances by the newest great West Indian batsman, the mercurial left-hander Brian Lara, and, ultimately, the surrender of the cherished

Frank Worrell Trophy to Australia. Richardson's initial Test as captain typified the fluctuating emotions that have engulfed West Indies cricket ever since.

It was a match of more than cricketing significance. It was against South Africa, a country previously beyond the pale of international sport because of its racially based apartheid policy. It was preceded by the World Cup where the inaugural meeting of the teams yielded victory to South Africa and the politically naive comment by Richardson that it was "just another cricket match". Along with the West Indies' elimination in the first round, the simmering row over the omission of Richards, Greenidge and Dujon and Marshall's biting statements, it led to an ugly reception for Richardson on his return home. He was booed the first time he led his team out in the Caribbean, in the one-day international at Sabina Park.

An embarrassing boycott of the one-off Test at Kensington Oval followed by Barbadians as incensed by the omission of Barbadian fast bowler Andy Cummins from the team as by the same issues that had so provoked the Jamaican crowds. It was an inauspicious start and when South Africa began the final day of the Test 122 for two in quest of a winning total of 201, it seemed certain ignominious defeat would be the final ingredient into the unappetising brew. It was then that the quality and the will power of Ambrose and Walsh were revealed. They were irresistible as the South Africans caved in, the last eight wickets tumbling to their intensity for 26 for a remarkable victory. It set a frequently repeated pattern.

When an unbeatable 2-0 lead and the Worrell Trophy were within Australia's grasp in the fourth Test in Adelaide later in 1992, Walsh conjured up the ball that ended their innings to clinch another heart-stopping triumph by a solitary run. In the decisive match at Perth a week later, Ambrose produced one of the most devastating spells in Test cricket history, sending back seven wickets for one run from 32 balls to set up an innings rout and a 2-1 series outcome. Back in the Caribbean, yet another awesome Ambrose burst was needed to stop England in their tracks at the Queen's Park Oval the following season.

After they played themselves into a position from which they required a feasible 194 to win, they were stunned by Ambrose's fire in the last 15 overs of the fourth afternoon. They ended the day 40 for eight and were 46 all out next morning, completing their third successive loss and guaranteeing another series success for the West Indies.

Two Tests later, at the Antigua Recreation Ground, Lara created history by surpassing the record score of another richly gifted West Indian left-hander, Garry Sobers, whose 365 not out against Pakistan 36 years earlier gave way to the new standard of 375. It brought instant fame and fortune to the engaging young Trinidadian who had announced himself to the cricketing world with a breathtaking 277 against Australia in Sydney just over a year earlier. The effect was profound and ultimately damaging.

It was Walsh's first Test as captain for Richardson and his deputy, Desmond Haynes, were both injured. By the end of the year, he was fully in charge on the tour of India as Richardson took the rest advised by his doctor – and once more the West Indies were obliged to pull the rabbit out of the hat to share the spoils. This time Walsh had a new accomplice. In the absence of Ambrose, who took the tour off, another Antiguan, Kenny Benjamin, had five wickets and Walsh three as India were swept aside for 114 in their second innings of the third and final Test, leaving the contest locked 1-1.

The magic could not last forever and the Australians, emerging as the game's new powerhouses, came to the Caribbean in 1995 to break the spell. The repercussions would be immediate and long-term. ◼

CAPTAINS Kepler Wessels of South Africa and Richie Richardson of the West Indies check on the toss for the inaugural Test between the teams at Kensington Oval to a background of empty seats. Upset by the omission of home town fast bowler Andy Cummins, Barbadians boycotted a historic match. The West Indies snatched a dramatic victory on the last day when the last eight South African wickets collapsed for 26 to Courtney Walsh and Curtly Ambrose, prompting the celebration of an Ambrose wicket with triumphant smiles and slap-stick high-fives.

THE arrest in Grenada of Pakistan's captain, Wasim Akram, and fast bowling colleague, Waqar Younis, on eventually dismissed charges of marijuana possession initially jeopardised the tour. It led to a new identification of Pakistan's Three Ws on the rails of the stand at Kensington named after the originals, Sir Frank Worrell, Sir Everton Weekes and Sir Clyde Walcott. On the field, an lbw decision brought contrasting reactions from batsman Inzamam-ul-Haq, bowler Ian Bishop and wicket-keeper Junior Murray.

THE meanest bowler on the field, a gentle giant off it, Curtly Ambrose takes time out with a young fan at the Antigua Recreation Ground where Carl Hooper compiled his highest match score in the final Test against Pakistan. His 178 not out was filled with typically graceful strokes such as his effortless hook.

ELATION for Pakistanis, despair for Trinidadians as Brian Lara is bowled off his pads four runs short of a century on his home ground, the Queen's Park Oval. Briefly bothered by problems with his eyes, the left-handed meastro needed attention from long-serving team trainer, the popular Australian, Dennis Waight.

A GREAT moment in history as Brian Lara leaves the Antigua Recreation Ground through an archway of bats formed by his teammates following his 375 against England. It was Test cricket's highest score and there to see his fellow West Indian left-hander surpass his previous mark of 365 not out, against Pakistan at Sabina Park in 1958, and greet him with a congratulatory hug was the great Sir Garry Sobers.

CRICKET and calypso are two, frequently intertwined cornerstones of Caribbean culture. Where there is one, there invariably will be the other and, as the West Indies neared victory over England at the Queen's Park Oval, four legendary calypsonians – from left, Chalkdust, Roaring Lion, Kitchener (on guitar) and Gypsy – were there to savour the occasion. In the following Test, at Kensington Oval, a delighted Winston Benjamin had Robin Smith caught at the wicket for 10.

THERE had never quite been a collapse like it in Test cricket in the West Indies. England set out on their quest to score a modest 194 to win the third Test at the Queen's Park Oval late on the fourth afternoon. By the close, they were 40 for eight, blown away by the irresistible Curtly Ambrose. Next morning they were all out for 46. Ambrose had six of the wickets - Mike Atherton lbw first ball (top left), Graham Thorpe whose off-stump was uprooted (top right); Jack Russell caught at slip (bottom right) and Robin Smith comprehensively bowled (right). One Test later, Alec Stewart scored hundreds in each innings of an England victory by 208 runs, the first West Indies defeat at Kensington since 1935.(bottom left)

IT was the season the Golden Era ended. After 15 years unbeaten in any Test series, the West Indies were defeated by Australia who came to the Caribbean and conquered 2-1. The die was cast in the first Test that Australia won by ten wickets. The disgruntled fan at Kensington Oval placed his feelings on a placard. In the middle, Jimmy Adams was a forlorn figure as he ran out of partners to be stranded 39 not out in West Indies' second innings.

AT the start of what was to be their own Golden Era, Australia were strong in every area, not least fielding. Steve Waugh's stunning catch to dismiss Junior Murray in the first Test typified the standard. Their exploits were followed by a sizeable group of supporters, at least one of whom found their team's success and the delights of the Caribbean an intoxicating mix.

IN a low-scoring series, batting was seldom the lark the quintessential No.11, Courtney Walsh, could make it out to be (above left). Brian Lara (far right) was the West Indies leading batsman but had his moments of anguish, and Richie Richardson (above right) only occasionally had a chance to indulge his favourite hook shot, as in his even 100 in the final Test.

NOWHERE was the intensity of the battle more vividly illustrated than in the eyeball-to-eyeball confrontation between Curtly Ambrose and Steve Waugh in the third Test at the Queen's Park Oval. After the Australian just avoided a throat-seeking bouncer, the two discussed the matter at close quarters, prompting captain Richie Richardson to intervene to end the conversation.

A PICTURE worth more than 1,000 words. Sorrow in the slips as Richie Richardson, Carl Hooper and Brian Lara contemplate the inevitability of a crushing Australian victory in the first Test at Kensington Oval.

ENGLAND'S new swing bowler, the bubbly Dominic Cork, undermined the West Indies in the summer's series with a match-winning seven for 43 at Lord's on debut and the first hat-trick for England in 38 years in the victory at Old Trafford. The strokeless Richie Richardson was the first in the sequence; Carl Hooper, the third, lbw.

# 1996-2000

WEST INDIES cricket has never known more turbulent and agonizing times than over the closing years of the 20th Century. There were four captains, four coaches and three managers in four years, each change contentious and unsettling. A self-styled "new dispensation" took over the West Indies board and immediately dropped the word "control" from its title. The paradoxical upshot was wrangling between the board and the players and within the board itself. A succession of administrative blunders compounded the problems.

Such chaos led to inevitable failure on the field, especially foreign fields. There were occasional flashes of brilliance to lighten the gloom but they were merely transient. In four successive overseas series – in Pakistan, South Africa, New Zealand and England - 13 of 15 Tests were lost, only one won. The Wisden Trophy was relinquished to England for the first time in 31 years.

Richie Richardson, harried throughout his four-year tenure as captain, quit two days before the board was to remove him following the shame of defeat by Kenya in the 1996 World Cup in India and Pakistan. Yet, within a week, he was leading his team into the semi-final.

Courtney Walsh took his place, as he had done earlier when Richardson was indisposed, even as a strong lobby was mounted for the promotion of Brian Lara. Walsh lasted two years before he was elbowed aside for Lara to assume the post for which he had long since been groomed. Lara himself, repeatedly the centre of the aggravation since his double record scores of 375 and 501 not out in 1994, had immediate success with a 3-1 series win over England in the Caribbean. But he soon found the pressure too great and packed it in after two years of what he termed "moderate success and devastating failure". The poisoned chalice passed on to Jimmy Adams but he, too, was an early victim.

The coaching job was handed on from Andy Roberts to Malcolm Marshall and, on Marshall's premature death, to Sir Viv Richards, all icons from an earlier era. When Roger Harper, a somewhat less commanding contemporary, was chosen instead of Richards in 2000, there were angry protests through the streets of Richards' native St.John's.

Wes Hall and Clive Lloyd, two of the West Indies' most celebrated cricketers of their time, were confronted by obstacles as managers that taxed their executive skills to the limit. Hall endured an especially difficult tour of England in 1995 when an agitated Lara had to be persuaded to rejoin the tour after storming out of a team meeting and announcing his retirement, Winston Benjamin was expelled and Curtly Ambrose, Kenny Benjamin, Carl Hooper and Lara all fined for disciplinary breaches.

A year later, Hall was gone to be succeeded by Lloyd. The highly successful and respected captain of the 1980s soon found himself in the middle of the players' strike prior to the 1998-99 tour of South Africa and, keener to coach than to manage, quit in 2000.

The election of Pat Rousseau, an energetic, high-profile Jamaican attorney and businessman, as board president was accompanied by much fanfare in 1996. Yet his strong-willed style of leadership soon lost him support and his climb-down in reinstating Lara as captain and Hooper as vice-captain after the players' strike weakened his position. Increasingly, the board over which he presided was criticised for its inability to properly handle even the most basic function, in spite of an increase in qualified personnel. Nothing was more embarrassing than when seven over-aged players were sent to the 1998 Youth World Cup in South Africa – unless it was the 1998 abandonment of the Sabina Park Test against England after 10.3 overs on account of a dangerous pitch. In light of such distractions, the team's abysmal record was hardly surprising.

What was extraordinary, even by the standards of which he had proved himself capable, was Lara's response to a couple of the many desperate points of his chequered career. At the height of the internal bickering that nearly precipitated an early end to his career in 1995, Lara returned to the fold and reeled off successive centuries in the last three Tests of a series drawn 2-2. Even more remarkable followed at home against Australia in 1999. When Lara returned from leading the West Indies to a 5-0 drubbing in South Africa, he was publicly castigated by the board for his "weaknesses in leadership" and placed on two Tests probation as captain. As the West Indies lost the first, bundled out for 51 at the Queen's Park Oval, his demise seemed certain. Instead, the captain saved himself, and his team, with match-winning scores of 213 at Sabina Park and 153 not out at Kensington to earn a share of the series with clearly superior opponents.

There was, still, the occasional throwback to the past from Ambrose and Walsh with a little help from the new fast bowlers whose turnover was faster even than that of captains and coaches. India were skittled for 81 when going after a mere 120 at Kensington Oval in 1997. Zimbabwe's collapse in the inaugural Test between the teams at the Queen's Park Oval in 2000 was even more sensational, 63 all out when set 99 for an historic win. Walsh set off wild and welcome celebrations at Sabina Park in Kingston, his home city, with Zimbabwe's last wicket, his 435th that sent him ahead of India's Kapil Dev as Test cricket's leading wicket-taker of all time.

It was a fitting reward for a tireless and committed campaigner in a struggling team. Perhaps what gave him as much satisfaction was his essential batting role as last man in one-wicket victories over Australia in 1999 and Pakistan the following year. These were rare successes. He and his illustrious partner, Ambrose, came into the team during the glorious years under Lloyd and Richards. They would bade their farewells in the disappointment of defeat. They, like Gordon Brooks, had experienced the good times and the bad. Like Gordon, they left us with everlasting memories. ■

JOYOUS times for the West Indies as flag-carrying fans at the Antigua Recreation Ground rush to hail Jimmy Adams' double-century against New Zealand in the second Test. The West Indies took the two - Test series 1-0 but such scenes, and results, were becoming increasingly few and far between.

GIVING new meaning to the term, Down Under, New Zealand captain Lee Germon indulges in a little unusual pre-match warm-up before the first Test in Barbados. But the kudos from the fan with the New Zealand flag were for Nathan Astle for his second innings 125, even if in a losing cause.

IT was officially billed as "The Decider" - and the 1996-97 series was decided 3-2 in Australia's favour. They set up their triumph with victory in the first Test in Brisbane where Shivnarine Chanderpaul's first innings dismissal triggered a collapse of the last seven wickets for 28. In the second innings, the desolate Sherwin Campbell could find no one to stay with him during his dogged second innings of 111.

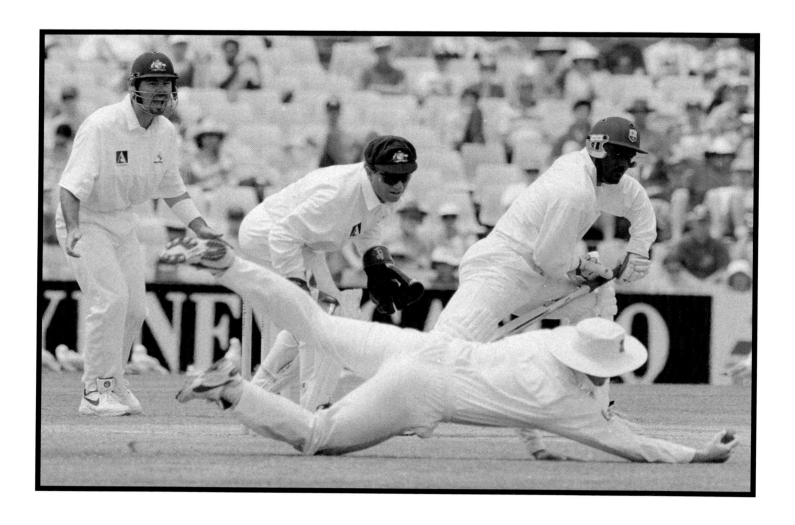

IT was Carl Hooper's best series as his 362 runs at an average of 45.25 led the West Indies batting. His 102 in the first Test in Brisbane was filled with confident strokes, such as the pull, and it took the remarkable reflexes and agility of Mark Taylor at slip to dislodge him for 57 in the second Test in Sydney.

WITH the West Indies down 2-0, Curtly Ambrose warmed up with a little football and then turned his attention to inspiring a three-day victory by six wickets before large crowds in the traditional Boxing Day Test at the Melbourne Cricket Ground. Among his nine wickets for 72 was Mark Waugh, lbw for 0 in Australia's first innings.

BACK in the Caribbean in 1997, the fans, and "Jumbo", the ebullient nut-seller at the Queen's Park Oval, could celebrate a West Indies series triumph over India and the arrival of an exciting new fast bowler, the Jamaican Franklyn Rose. His six wickets in his debut innings before his home crowd at Sabina Park included the thrilling sight of Sachin Tendulkar's flying off-stump.

IN a decision unprecedented in the long history of the game, the umpires declared the Sabina Park pitch too dangerous and abandoned the first Test of the series against England after 10.1 overs. By then, England captain Mike Atherton had to jack-knife to avoid Curtly Ambrose's bouncer, and Alec Stewart was left in hands-a-kimbo bemusement after another delivery flew over keeper David Williams' head for four byes.

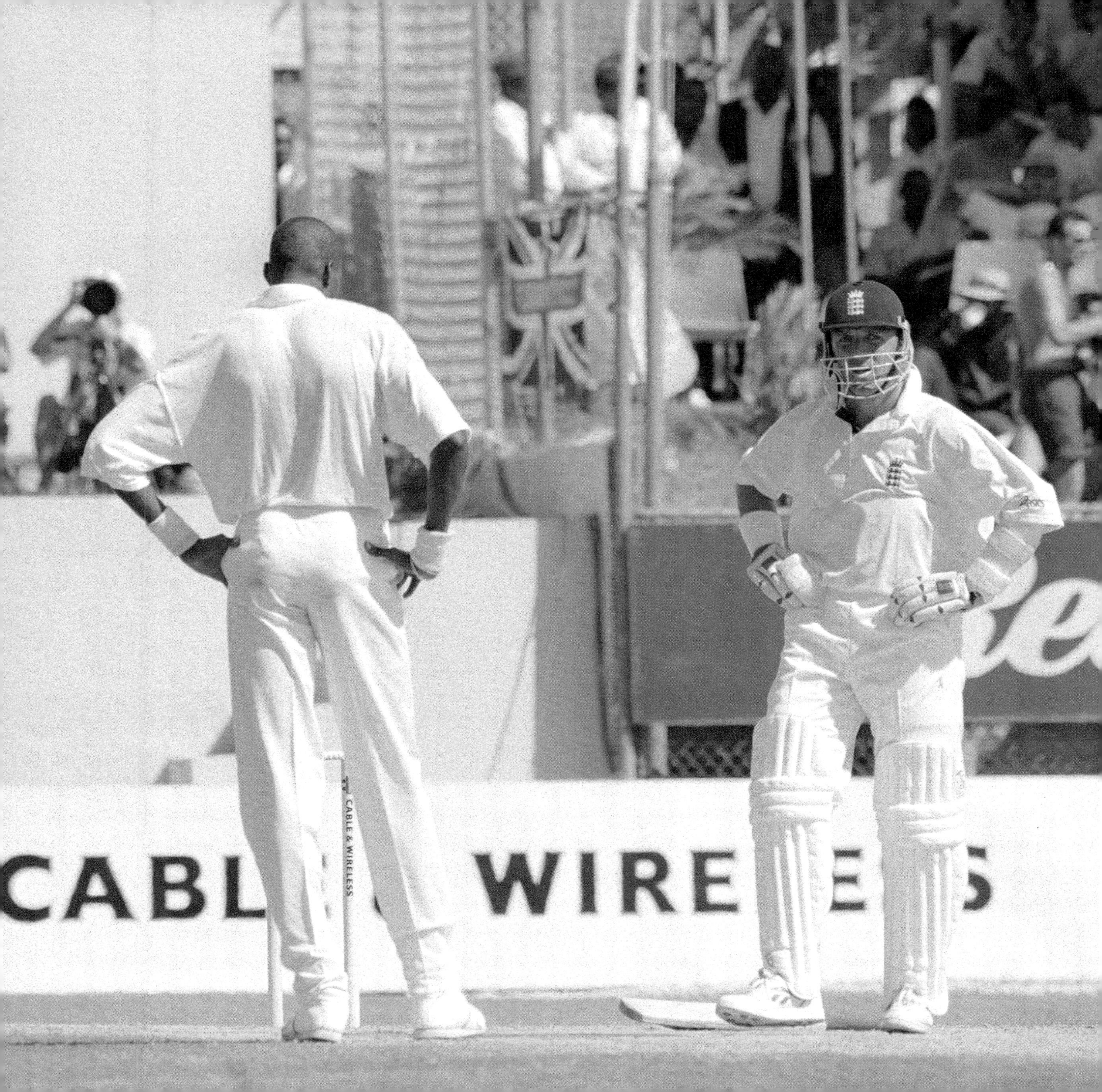
CABLE & WIRELESS

AN ashen-faced Atherton walks from the ground after he was out to Walsh in the Sabina debacle, returning to the sanctuary of the team's dug-out to watch the unfolding drama behind sunglasses, in company with Nasser Hussain, another one of the three wickets.

DAVID WILLIAMS is yorked by Andy Caddick (above left) and Brian Lara caught by wicket-keeper Jack Russell off Angus Fraser (above right) in England's only win in the series in the third Test at the Queen's Park Oval. The 3-1 outcome was formalised by Clayton Lambert's tumbling short-leg catch to dismiss Phil Tufnell off Courtney Walsh that completed the West Indies' victory in the final Test.

SHIVNARINE Chanderpaul has Mark Ramprekash taking cover in the final Test. His 118 in the fourth Test at Bourda was the first hundred by a Guyanese in front of his home crowd since 1973 and helped set up a West Indies win. The series-clinching result in the final Test at the Antigua Recreation Ground delighted West Indians, none more so than Curtly Ambrose and Dinanath Ramnarine.

THERE was little joy, plenty of pain, literal and figurative, on the first full tour of South Africa in 1998-99 that resulted in a 5-0 whitewash in the Test series. Courtney Walsh's elation at surpassing Malcolm Marshall's West Indies record 376 Test wickets in the first Test in Johannesburg was overridden by a spate of injuries. The first put Jimmy Adams out of the tour after he mysteriously sliced tendons in his left hand on the flight from London.

TEN LITTLE WINDIANS
BATTING IN THE SUN
KASPA, PISTOL, WARNE, M°GRATH....
AND THEN THERE WERE NONE!

SIGNS OF THE TIMES (1): Unsympathetic sentiments that reflected West Indies' declining fortunes in Australia in 1996-97 (above) and South Africa (right) in 1998-99. Yet, as at Centurion in South Africa, they still attracted the crowds.

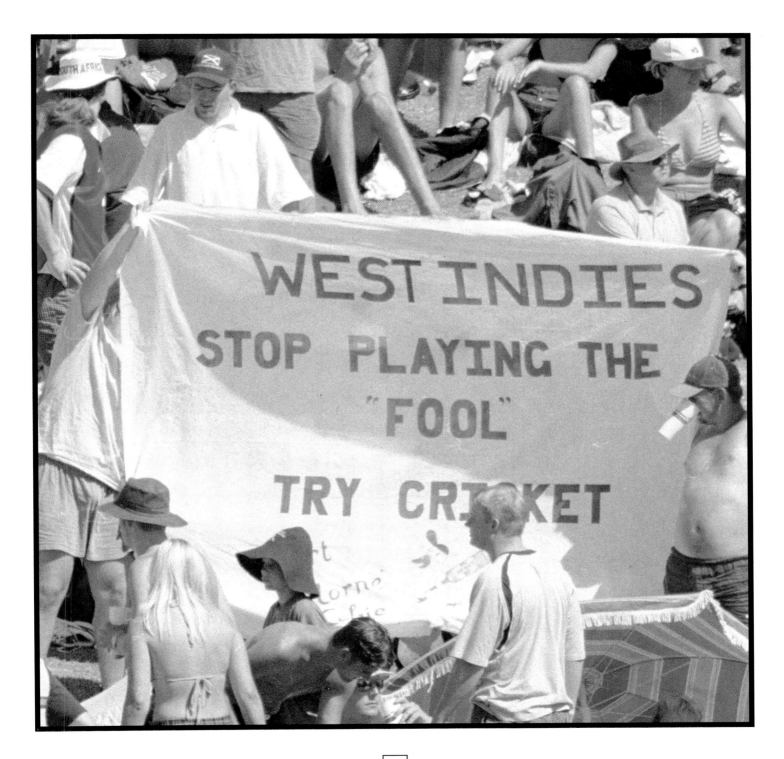

SIGNS OF THE TIMES (2): The urging on the sightscreen in South Africa in 1998-99 couldn't inspire captain Brian Lara and manager Clive Lloyd whose distress was evident at the final press conference. But, back in the Caribbean, Lara responded with three inspiring performances that led the West Indies to an unexpected 2-2 share of the series with Australia. After his match-winning 213 at Sabina neither the security personnel nor jubilant fans could keep up with him as he sprinted from the ground.

LARA'S momentous innings in Barbados defied Australia's bowlers, wicket-keeper Ian Healy's between-the-legs attempt to run him out and the perimeter advertising slogan to remain unbeaten on 153 with brilliant stroke play to secure a breathtaking victory by one wicket.

THE withering stare of debutant fast bowler Corey Collymore followed a bouncer that whizzed past Mark Waugh's nose. But the more appropriate expressions in the final Test at the Antigua Recreation Ground were on West Indian faces in the crowd as defeat allowed Australia to level the series 2-2 and retain the Frank Worrell Trophy.

 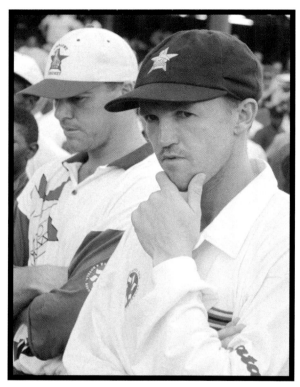

BROTHERS Grant (left) and Andy Flower expressed their disappointment differently as Zimbabwe capitulated to 63 all out and defeat at the Queen's Park Oval in the West Indies' first Test of the millennium. Batsmen were embarrassed in more ways than one in a low-scoring match. Shivnarine Chanderpaul's stance, when lbw in the second innings, was open to several interesting interpretations.

Randy Brooks

ZIMBABWE'S last man, Henry Olonga, plays forward, Wavell Hinds sticks out a long left-hand to snap up the catch at short-leg and history, and instant bedlam, is created. As he surpasses Kapil Dev's 434 as Test cricket's leading wicket-taker Courtney Walsh rewards Hinds with an euphoric embrace, and his home pitch at Sabina Park with a ceremonial kiss.

CONTRASTING fortunes for two West Indian icons. While Brian Lara was enmeshed in such "concern about my cricketing future" that he quit the captaincy and took a break from the game prior to the home series against Zimbabwe and Pakistan, Viv Richards was accorded a knighthood by the government of his native Antigua and Barbuda. Appropriately, he was dubbed Sir Vivian by Governor-General Sir James Carlisle in an on-field ceremony at the Antigua Recreation Ground during the Pakistan Test.

PAKISTAN'S off-spinner Saqlain Mushtaq breached Sherwin Campbell's defence in the drawn second Test at Kensington Oval. But Courtney Walsh, in his own inimitable style (above) and through a lucky escape off a close-in catch (left), held on with captain Jimmy Adams to claim a tense, one-wicket win in the final Test that decided the series 1-0.

THE 50th anniversary of the West Indies' first Test victory in England brought a parade of several survivors of the 1950 triumph at Lord's from both sides, among them two of the legendary Three Ws, Sir Clyde Walcott and Sir Everton Weekes. But it turned into a West Indian nightmare, the scoreboard recording their lowest total in a Test against England, and an England victory proclaimed by Dominic Cork after he hit the winning runs off Courtney Walsh.

CAMPBELL   c GOUGH b CADDICK   4
GRIFFITH   c STEWART b GOUGH   1
HINDS   c RAMP'KASH b CADDIC   0
LARA   c CORK b CADDICK   5
CHAN'PAUL   c RAMP'KASH b GOUGH   9
ADAMS   lbw b CORK   3
JACOBS   c ATHERTON b CADDICK   12
AMBROSE   c RAMP'KASH b CADDIC   0
ROSE   c & b CORK   1
KING   lbw b CORK   7
WALSH   3
                                        9

WEST INDIES   54/10 EXTRAS

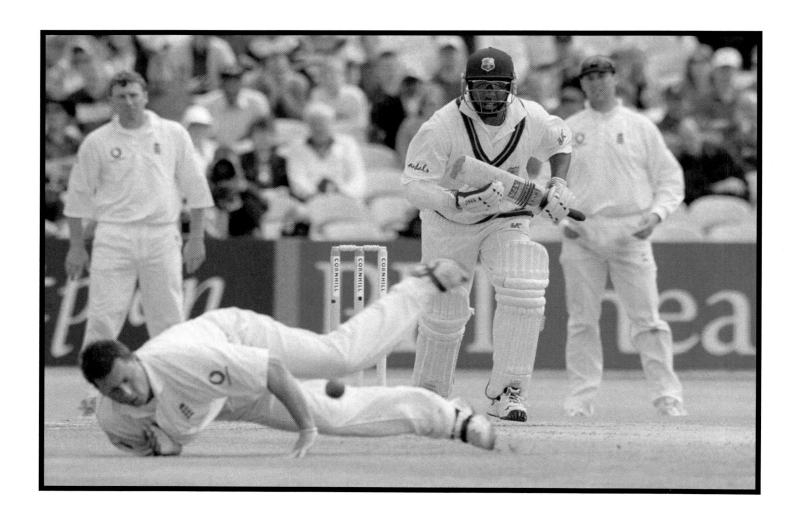

NOTABLE West Indian performances were uncommon in a summer in which the Wisden Trophy was ceded back to England. But Brian Lara limboed and on-drove his way to 112 at Old Trafford, the West Indies' only hundred of the series.
(Overleaf) Curtly Ambrose snared his 400th Test victim at Headingley, fittingly Mike Atherton caught at slip. One match later, at the Oval, Ambrose waved his good-byes to Test cricket after a dozen years and 405 wickets.

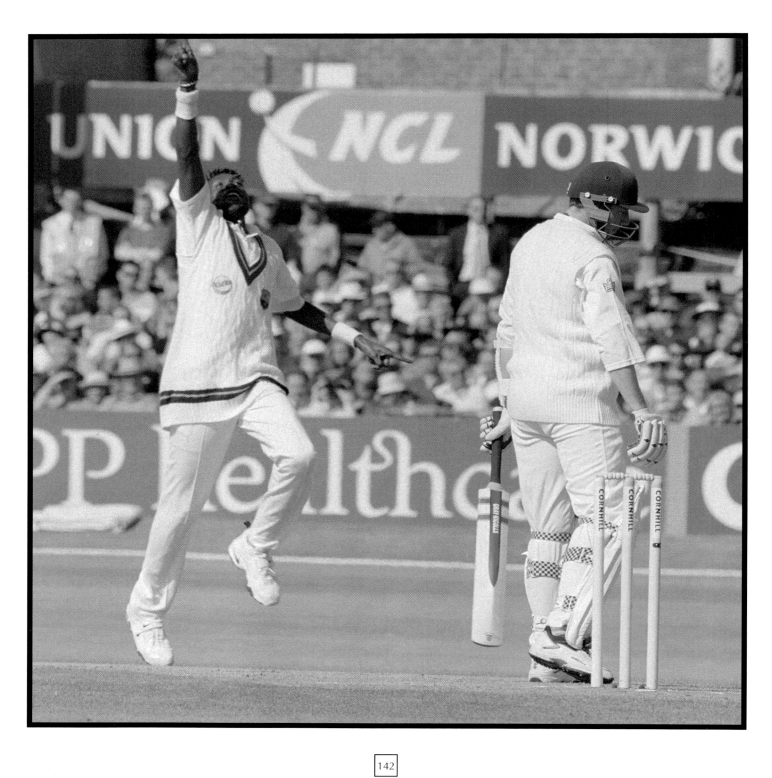